HERBERT *Hoover*

HERBERT *Hoover*

OUR THIRTY-FIRST PRESIDENT

By Gerry and Janet Souter

SPIRIT
of America™

The Child's World®, Inc.
Chanhassen, Minnesota

HERBERT *Hoover*

Published in the United States of America by The Child's World®, Inc.
PO Box 326 • Chanhassen, MN 55317-0326 • 800-599-READ • www.childsworld.com

Acknowledgments

The Creative Spark: Mary Francis-DeMarois, Project Director; Elizabeth Sirimarco Budd, Series Editor; Robert Court, Design and Art Direction; Janine Graham, Page Layout; Jennifer Moyers, Production

The Child's World®, Inc.: Mary Berendes, Publishing Director; Red Line Editorial, Fact Research; Cindy Klingel, Curriculum Advisor; Robert Noyed, Historical Advisor

Photos

Cover: White House Collection, courtesy White House Historical Association; Bettmann/Corbis: 28, 29, 31, 36; Corbis: 11, 24; Courtesy of the Herbert Hoover Library, West Branch, IA: 6, 7, 8, 9, 10, 12, 13, 14, 15, 17, 18, 21, 22, 26, 33, 34, 36, 37; The Library of Congress: 16, 19, 20, 27, 30

Registration

The Child's World®, Inc., Spirit of America™, and their associated logos are the sole property and registered trademarks of The Child's World®, Inc.

Library of Congress Cataloging-in-Publication Data

Souter, Gerry.
  Herbert Hoover, our thirty-first president / by Gerry and Janet Souter.
    p. cm.
  Includes bibliographical references and index.
  ISBN 1-56766-865-8
  1. Hoover, Herbert, 1874–1964—Juvenile literature. 2. Presidents—United
States—Biography—Juvenile literature. [1. Hoover, Herbert, 1874–1964. 2. Presidents.]
I. Souter, Janet, 1940–   . II. Title.
  E802 .S7 2001
  973.91'6'092—dc21

                                                              00-011492

16   22   34

Contents

Chapter ONE

A Religious Childhood

Herbert Hoover, shown here at age three, spent his early years in Iowa. He enjoyed hiking, exploring, and swimming. He spent as much time as he could outdoors.

ON AUGUST 10, 1874, HERBERT CLARK Hoover was born in the town of West Branch, Iowa. It was a small town with plain houses. There were no fancy shops or businesses, but the town did have a meetinghouse where religious services were held.

Herbert, the cheerful second son of Jesse and Hulda Hoover, was nicknamed "Bertie." Religion was important to Bertie's family. There were prayer meetings in the Hoover home, and the family went to church meetings in town twice a week. This gave young Herbert "strong training in patience," as he later remembered. His parents had a third child in 1876.

Herbert's father was a blacksmith, making and repairing horseshoes and other iron goods.

Jesse Hoover (at left) moved to Iowa with his father in 1854. They traveled by riverboat and covered wagon to get there and settled in the town of West Branch.

In 1878, he began manufacturing farm equipment. The business was successful. Sadly, Jesse became ill just two years later. He died in 1880 at the age of 34. Hulda did her best to keep the family together. She took in sewing and rented out a room in their house.

After Jesse's death, religion became even more important to the Hoover family. They belonged to the Quaker religion, which is a

Herbert's mother, Hulda Minthorn Hoover, was originally from Ontario, Canada. She was a school teacher in West Branch when she met Jesse Hoover. She was also a Quaker minister and taught Sunday school. She enjoyed writing poems and songs for her students.

Christian faith. Quakers believe strongly in the values of hard work and honesty. Both men and women can be leaders in the church. In 1883, Herbert's mother became a minister. She traveled throughout Iowa, preaching and holding prayer meetings. Relatives cared for the Hoover children while she was away.

Tragedy struck the Hoover family again in 1884, when Hulda died of typhoid fever. The children were separated and sent to live with relatives. Herbert lived with his Uncle Allan. Herbert's older brother, Tad, stayed with another uncle, while Hulda's mother raised their sister, May. For a year and a half, Herbert enjoyed farm life with his Uncle Allan's family. In November of 1885, another uncle, Doctor John Minthorn, asked that Herbert come to live with him in Oregon after his own son had died. With only a few coins in his pocket and some food prepared by his aunt, Herbert boarded a train for Newberg, Oregon.

John Minthorn ran a strict household. He insisted that young Herbert milk cows, gather firewood, and feed and water the horses. When Herbert was 14 years old, the family moved to the town of Salem, Oregon. His uncle opened a real estate office, and Herbert worked there for two years.

While working in his uncle's office, Herbert met many different types of people. One man worked as an engineer, making his living by designing new and better ways to do things. Herbert often spoke to the engineer and was curious about this work. A woman in the neighborhood convinced Herbert to take business classes at a nearby school.

When he was 17, Herbert decided to study engineering at college. Stanford University in Northern California had

The Hoover children were separated after their mother's death left them orphaned. Each went to live with different relatives. Herbert (at right) eventually went to live in Oregon with the Minthorn family.

▶ Being raised in the Quaker religion meant that the Hoover boys could not carry guns. They learned to hunt with bows and arrows instead.

▶ Hoover had a scar on the bottom of his foot throughout his life. He got it as a child when he walked into his father's blacksmith shop barefooted and stepped on a glowing ember.

just opened and was looking for students. Herbert took the entrance exam that determined whether he would be admitted to the school. He did very well in math. Even though he hadn't yet finished high school, he was accepted to Stanford. It looked as if he had the talent to become an engineer.

Hoover was accepted to Stanford University. He was a member of the "pioneer class," the very first graduating class from the school. He is shown here, seated at left, with other engineering students.

THE QUAKER RELIGION influenced Hoover's actions throughout his life. Quakers call themselves "Friends of the Truth," or simply "Friends." Living their faith means striving for peace and helping people who are less fortunate, especially those who are victims of an unjust law or way of life. The Friends are great believers in education and have a keen interest in world affairs. They believe their mission is to make the world a better place to live. Friends also must strive throughout their lives to be good and decent. This photograph shows President and Mrs. Hoover leaving the Friends Meeting House in Washington, D.C., while he was president.

Friends believe a person, no matter how poor, should find some way to earn a living, rather than depend on the charity of others. Hoover remembered this philosophy all his life. He did what he could to help people, but he expected them to help themselves as well. An admirer of Hoover once said that if a man asked the president for a dime, he would not give it to him. But he would put him in touch with an agency that could find him work.

Chapter TWO

Engineer and World Traveler

Lou Henry was the only female geology student in Herbert's class at Stanford. The two young people had a great deal in common and soon fell in love.

WHILE AT STANFORD, HERBERT HOOVER became fascinated with geology, the study of Earth's rocks and minerals. He decided to become a mining engineer. A woman named Lou Henry was also studying engineering at Stanford. She was strong and smart. She and Hoover had a lot in common. They had been born within 100 miles of each other in Iowa. They were both geology majors, and they both loved to fish. Herbert and Lou made plans to marry as soon as he was able to support her.

To earn money, Hoover worked nights in a California gold mine. It was hard, back-breaking work, but it helped him to better understand his profession. Working in the mine taught him things he never could have

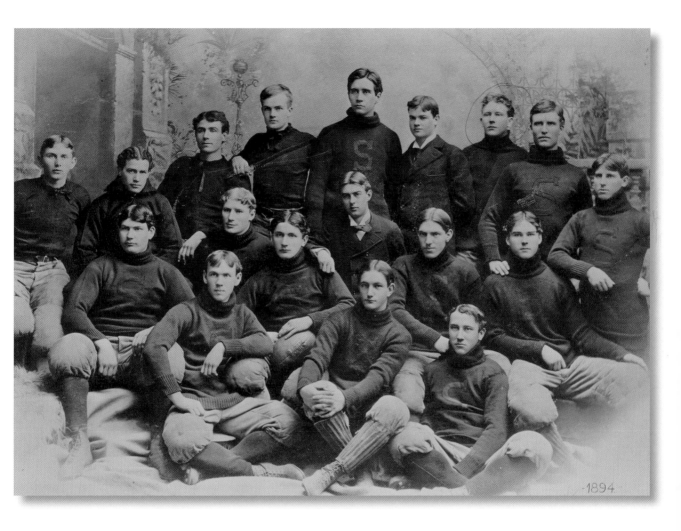

-1894

learned from a book. Later, Hoover found a job in the office of a mining engineering company in San Francisco. His hard work eventually led to a job with Bewick, Moreing and Company, a British engineering firm.

The company sent 22-year-old Hoover to Australia. He spent long hours in 100-degree weather, inspecting mines and searching for gold. He excelled at his work and helped the company earn a lot of money. Hoover was

At Stanford, Hoover was manager of the football team. He is shown here in the back row, third from the right.

13

quite successful himself, earning $12,500 per year. Although that was a great deal of money at that time, it did not make him happy. Hoover was lonely. "Anyone who envies me my salary can … take my next trip with me," he once said. "He would be contented to be a bank clerk." Herbert longed to return home. He called the town in Australia where he lived "a place of red dust, black flies, and white heat … one of the hottest, driest, and dustiest places on this Earth."

Hoover is shown here during the time he lived in Australia. There he worked for Bewick, Moreing and Company, helping them determine the value of mines in the region.

14

In 1899, Hoover returned to the United States with one purpose— to marry Lou Henry. By then she also had graduated from Stanford with a degree in geology. The day they were married, they left for Tientsin, a small province in China where Hoover would work as a mining engineer. Foreigners were not welcome in China at that time. Many Chinese believed that the science and engineering of the West would hurt their country. They also worried that Westerners would bring Christianity to China, destroying their own traditional religions. These **rebels,** known as the Boxers, wanted to keep out all things foreign. The Chinese government continued to make agreements with other nations, however.

A conflict broke out that turned into a war known as the Boxer Rebellion. The Boxers planned to destroy every foreign thing in China—railways, telegraphs, houses, and people. The rebellion began in June of 1900. The Hoovers were trapped in Tientsin until August. Heavy bombing and gun-fire were all around them. Finally, they were able to leave for England on a German mail boat.

The Hoovers lived in Tientsin, China, for about one year. Herbert began taking lessons to learn the Chinese language shortly after they arrived. He is shown here with his Chinese teacher.

Interesting Facts

▶ From China, Lou Hoover sent letters home asking for clothing that they couldn't buy in Tientsin. She also asked for books and magazines because she and Herbert loved to read.

Soldiers from many countries tried to stop the Boxer Rebellion. Here Japanese soldiers are shown in battle against the Boxers.

After the rebellion ended, the Hoovers returned to China, and Herbert returned to work at the mine.

Hoover felt that the Chinese should be allowed to make some of the mining decisions. The director of Bewick, Moreing and Company strongly disagreed. He wanted total control of the business. This disagreement finally forced the Hoovers to leave China.

16

Herbert continued to work for the company, traveling to other parts of the world. The Hoovers' first child was born in London on August 4, 1903. They named him Herbert Clark Jr. For the next few years, the Hoovers brought their young son along on their travels. In 1907, they welcomed their second son, Allan. The following year, Hoover left Bewick, Moreing and Company and returned to the United States. Mrs. Hoover wanted to raise their children at home.

Hoover formed his own engineering company in 1908. He soon became known as "the Great Engineer." His company had several offices, including sites in London, New York, and San Francisco.

During the Boxer Rebellion, the Hoovers were once trapped in their home while bullets sprayed around them. This room in their home was pockmarked by bullet holes.

AT THE TIME LOU HENRY GRADUATED FROM STANFORD, MOST WOMEN IN the United States hadn't finished high school, much less received a degree in geology. Lou Henry was not like most women. Before she was born, her father had dreamed of all the things he could do if he had a son. When his wife had a baby girl, he decided they could still have fun together. Mr. Henry took Lou with him to do all the things he enjoyed. They fished, took hunting trips, and went camping, even though it was more common in those days for boys to enjoy these pastimes. Mr. Henry also taught Lou about nature and the outdoors. She was also an excellent athlete. When people called her a tomboy, Lou didn't mind one bit.

After she married Herbert, Lou Hoover traveled all over the world with him. In fact, they departed for China on the very afternoon of their wedding. She was

always ready for an
adventure. In the
photograph at left, she
is shown with one of
the cannons that fired
on the town of
Tientsin during the
Boxer Rebellion.

As first lady, Mrs.
Hoover was known for
her kind treatment of the
servants and staff who worked at
the White House. When employ-
ees were ill, she had food sent to them
from the White House kitchen. She saw to
it that a White House butler was given proper medical treatment when
he had tuberculosis, a serious disease of the lungs.

Lou Hoover believed all people should be treated equally. She was as
polite to girl scouts who visited the White House as she was to important
politicians. Once she invited Mrs. Oscar De Priest to tea at the White House.
Mrs. De Priest was an African American, the wife of a black congressman. At
the time, some people still believed that blacks should not be guests at the
White House. That day, some guests refused to shake hands with Mrs. De
Priest. But Lou did everything she could to make the woman feel at ease.

Chapter THREE

The Humanitarian

Hoover had great success as a businessman. This allowed him to volunteer his time to help people. He rarely accepted a salary for his efforts.

IN JUNE OF 1914, WORLD WAR I BEGAN WHEN the countries of Germany and Austria-Hungary went to war against England, France, and Russia. Hoover was working in England at the time. American officials asked him to help get money and clothing for Americans stranded in London. Hoover raised more than a million dollars to help the 120,000 American citizens there. He soon became known as a **humanitarian** because he dedicated his time to helping others.

Shortly after, Hoover heard about the terrible conditions in Belgium. Germany had taken over the tiny country. Now it refused to supply food for the Belgian people. There was not enough land for farming in Belgium. Its citizens depended on other nations to supply their food. What little farmland there was

The German army destroyed many Belgian towns during World War I. This left many citizens starving and homeless. Hoover wanted to help, so he created the Committee for Relief of Belgium.

had been destroyed during the war, and the people were starving. Hoover knew he had to do something. But how could he gather a food supply large enough to feed more than 10 million people every day? And how would he get the food to Belgium?

Hoover went to the war-torn country and formed a group called the Committee for Relief of Belgium. He raised money for food and arranged for transportation to take it to the people who needed it. Although there were many problems with this operation, Hoover handled them well. He did such a good job that when the United States entered

Hoover's efforts during World War I saved millions of European children.

the war, the government asked him to take on a similar role for his own country.

Hoover returned to the United States in 1917 to form the U.S. Food Administration. It was responsible for supplying food to American soldiers and to their **allies,** the British and French soldiers. The U.S. Food Administration also had to make sure there was enough food for U.S. citizens and the citizens of England and France. This was a difficult job, but Hoover never took any pay for it. He directed this operation with great care. He set up a food **conservation** plan. This included a system for storing wheat when it was plentiful and releasing it when it was scarce. An important part of Hoover's plan involved Americans at home. If people did not waste food, extra supplies could be sent to help soldiers and citizens overseas. The Food Administration asked Americans to make sacrifices and save food. Posters and signs told Americans that "Food Will Win the War" and "When in Doubt, Serve Potatoes."

Americans were asked to have "meatless Mondays" and "wheatless Wednesdays." This type of conservation became known as "Hooverizing." Hoover wanted these actions to be voluntary. He didn't believe that the government should tell people what to do. He felt a **democracy** depended on the strength of each citizen. This belief stayed with him all his life, and people cooperated, both in the United States and in Europe.

Hoover's job of feeding the hungry did not end once the war was over in 1918. The Committee for Relief of Belgium and the Food Administration worked together to help

The Home Conservation Division helped encourage Americans to "Hooverize," or conserve food during the war effort.

both America's allies and its former enemies, the Germans. Germany faced terrible problems at the end of World War I. President Woodrow Wilson asked Hoover to help Germans and other Europeans begin planting and then harvesting crops. People criticized Hoover for helping the enemy. But he felt that people—especially children—should not be left to starve. "Twenty million people are starving," he said, "whatever their **politics** they should be fed." He asked the Friends Service Committee, a Quaker organization, to lead separate operations for Germany. After the war, the American Relief Administration fed 350 million people in 21 countries.

Hoover's work in Europe was finished in 1919, and he gladly returned home. He was now so well known that people from both of the major **political parties,** the Democrats and the Republicans, thought he should run for president. But Hoover wanted a quiet life. He and Lou built a home in California near Stanford University. Lou designed their house herself. The family prepared to settle into a quiet life at home.

Hoover didn't remain idle for long, however. Between 1919 and 1921, he made 46 speeches and wrote more than 50 magazine articles. He also led conferences and spoke before Congress.

Warren Harding was elected president in 1920. He named Hoover the secretary of **commerce.** In this position, Hoover advised the president on business matters. At the time, this was not considered a time-consuming position. It took up only a few hours of the secretary's day. But Hoover was not content with such a small position. He expanded the agency and made it a vital part of the government. Under Hoover's direction, the Commerce Department began to offer

Lou Hoover designed the Hoover family home in Palo Alto, California.

more advice and information to help businesses around the country. He took steps to increase regulations that would make workplaces safer. He also encouraged businesses to produce their products in uniform sizes. All companies that made items such as light bulbs, paper, or nuts and bolts would produce them in the same size. This way, parts from different companies could work together.

Children's health was still an important issue for Hoover. He wanted all American children to receive **vaccinations** against disease. He also encouraged the government to provide milk and hot lunches to poor children.

As the secretary of commerce, Hoover led the way to make **technology** a driving force in the United States. **Aviation** was a new and exciting field. Hoover thought that airplanes could be used to deliver mail more quickly. He encouraged airport crews to install lights on runways to make takeoffs and landings safer. Television was first demonstrated during this period. In fact, the first public demonstration of television featured Herbert Hoover.

Hoover, standing second from right, is shown here with President Harding's cabinet. Harding is seated third from right. Hoover was the secretary of commerce. He hoped to improve the way Americans did business and immediately set to work to accomplish his goals.

The 1920s were a period of growth and **prosperity.** Many industries reduced the workday to eight hours, giving people more time off. Because wages were high and the **economy** was strong, many people purchased goods on a "payment plan." This meant they bought goods and paid for them a little at a time, a system similar to the credit cards people use today. Everyone thought these good times would go on forever.

Hoover (seated) was pictured on the first transmission of television signals on April 7, 1927. He spoke to and was seen by the president of the American Telephone and Telegraph Company in New York City.

HOOVER WAS SUCCESSFUL IN PROVIDING FOOD AND CLOTHING FOR VICTIMS OF World War I because he was allowed to make all decisions for the operation. In November of 1918, President Woodrow Wilson put Hoover in charge of helping feed the starving people in post-war Europe. Hoover knew the people needed nourishing food to rebuild their nations. In fact, he asked President Wilson for the job, knowing he was the best person to accomplish this difficult task.

Hoover established operation headquarters in Paris. He began by taking charge of railroads, river transportation, and communications. He renewed coal production to keep homes and factories warm. He provided medical care to eliminate diseases that had run rampant during the war.

Hoover returned home in 1919, proud of his accomplishments. His organization had supplied nearly 20 nations with food, clothing, seeds for planting, and other supplies. His caring nature and his skills had fed millions of people all over the world.

Chapter FOUR

A Troubled Presidency

Hoover was ready to run for president in 1928, and he won the election. Unfortunately, the nation stood at the brink of a difficult period. His would be a long, painful presidency.

IN 1928, HOOVER RAN FOR THE NATION'S highest office—the presidency. His opponent was Alfred Smith, a member of the Democratic Party. Hoover was a Republican, and the nation had enjoyed success with the last two Republican presidents. People had confidence in their leadership, and Hoover easily won the election.

Herbert Hoover's **inauguration** took place on March 4, 1929. It was the first time Americans could hear the ceremony on the radio. His early days in office promised good times and a bright future for the country. President Hoover started many major building projects, including the Hoover Dam near Las Vegas, Nevada, and the Grand Coulee Dam in the state of Washington. He added five million

acres of land to the national forest and park system. This land was set aside for recreation and conservation of the nation's wilderness.

Hoover reduced taxes for families with low **incomes.** Farmers around the country were having a difficult time earning a living. Hoover created the Federal Farm Board. It helped them earn more money for their crops by raising prices. It also worked to sell more produce to other countries.

Less than a year after Hoover entered office, the good times ended. October 29, 1929, is known as "Black Friday." It is the day the **stock market** crashed. The value of

Interesting Facts

▶ Hoover believed that children were America's hope for the future. "If we could have but one generation of properly born, trained, educated and healthy children, a thousand other problems of government would vanish," he once said.

a company is largely based on the price people are willing to pay for its stock, which are shares of the company. When stock is sold cheaply, the company is considered to be worth less than when prices are high.

Many **investors** in the 1920s bought stock with money they borrowed from banks. They hoped that stock prices would rise. If that happened, they would make a **profit.** From that profit, investors planned to pay back the money they borrowed. For a few years, this worked. But at the end of the decade, many companies began to lose money. This lowered the price of stock. Investors did not make the profits they hoped they would. Then they could not repay the money they had borrowed. Many banks went out of business when investors couldn't repay their loans. People who had savings in these banks lost their money as well.

Companies lost money when stock prices fell. They had to fire many employees. Without jobs, no one could afford to buy the products companies made. This made American businesses lose even more money. This difficult period in history is known as the "Great Depression."

Times were tough for the rest of Hoover's presidency. Each year, farmers received less money for their crops. Even the Federal Farm Board was unable to help. Banks had very little money. The people who did have jobs were afraid of losing them. No matter what ideas Hoover had, he had no support from Congress or from American businesses.

Hoover created the Reconstruction Finance Corporation (RFC) in 1932. Its purpose was to loan money to businesses that were vital to the nation's economy. The RFC also loaned money to state and local governments. Unfortunately, this did little to help the economy. Still, Hoover believed that people should not expect the government to give them money. "I am confident that our people have the resources … to meet this situation in the way they have met their problems over generations." He meant that Americans had always had the ability to solve their own problems without help from

A policeman stood guard outside the entrance to New York's World Exchange Bank in 1931. Frightened customers stormed U.S. banks during the Great Depression, trying to take out their savings. Unfortunately, many banks had lost all their money, leaving people penniless.

People who lost their homes were forced to live in make-shift shacks in shantytowns. People called these towns "Hoovervilles," blaming the president for their hardships.

the government. He did not believe that should change, even in a severe crisis such as a depression. This belief made people angry. Many without jobs had to live in cardboard shack settlements. These became known as "Hoovervilles."

Although Hoover still believed that the Great Depression would be over soon, things only grew worse. In his last year of office, Hoover began new government programs to provide for hungry Americans. He also tried to help the banks. But most Americans thought Hoover hadn't done enough—and that he had waited too long to do what little he did.

Democrat Franklin Delano Roosevelt easily beat Hoover in the election of 1932. Roosevelt's outgoing personality made Americans trust him. He promised to help people. Hoover felt that voters had judged him unfairly. "I had little hope of reelection in 1932," he wrote. "One of Roosevelt's most effective campaign issues was to allege that I had made the Depression and then done nothing about it."

After President Hoover left office, he and Mrs. Hoover returned to their California home. They later had an apartment in New York City as well. For many years, they led a quiet life, although the nation struggled with the Depression and then with World War II. The Hoovers enjoyed fishing, reading, and spending time with their family.

In 1944, Lou Henry Hoover died suddenly of a heart attack. President Roosevelt died the following year. His vice president, Harry Truman, became president. Truman remembered Hoover's talents and soon put them to use. In 1946, Europeans were devastated by World War II. Truman asked Hoover to help them recover. In 1947, Truman asked Hoover to lead a committee to make the U.S. government work more smoothly and efficiently. This position continued under President Eisenhower. During this time, Hoover also wrote several books.

Herbert Hoover is shown here with homeless Polish children in the city of Warsaw. President Truman sent Hoover as a special representative to help war-torn Europe in 1946, just after World War II had ended. Hoover's job was to study and help solve the critical food shortage, just as he had done after World War I.

By the early 1960s, Hoover's health was failing. He attended the opening of the Hoover Presidential Library and Museum in West Branch, Iowa, in 1962. But when he returned to New York, he became quite ill. Herbert Hoover died on October 20, 1964. He was 90 years old.

Hoover is most often remembered as the president who failed to rescue the nation from the Great Depression. But later in his life, people remembered all the good he had done. He worked hard to see that food was provided for both Americans and Europeans during wartime. He also promoted science and industry.

The Great Depression challenged all the nation's leaders. Perhaps Herbert Hoover could have been a great president in different times, for he loved his country and its people. "Within the soul of America is freedom of mind and spirit," he once said. "Perhaps it's not perfect, but it's more full of its realization than any other place in the world."

Hoover attended the dedication of the Hoover Presidential Library and Museum in West Branch. It took place on his 88th birthday and was one of his last public appearances.

THE U.S. CONGRESS promised to give **veterans** of World War I a $1,000 bonus for their efforts, but they had to wait until 1945 to collect it. In 1932, the country was suffering from the Great Depression. The veterans needed their bonus money immediately to feed and clothe their families. A group of veterans decided to go to Washington and demand their bonus money. They became known as the Bonus Army.

President Hoover knew that the government did not yet have the money to pay the former soldiers. By June, more than 20,000 people had arrived in Washington. Hoover would not give in to their demands, but he did provide the people with blankets, food, and medical supplies.

The veterans' demands were ignored for several weeks, and their presence became a serious problem. They begged for food and asked strangers for money. Police tried to force them to leave, but they refused. A riot broke out, and Hoover asked General Douglas MacArthur to break up the disturbance.

The general gathered 800 soldiers. Hoover only wanted MacArthur's troops to send the rioters back to their campsites. But the troops threw tear-gas bombs to break up the mob. Hoover ordered MacArthur to leave them alone. The general refused, sending his soldiers into the camp with orders to burn everything. The veterans left, taking what little they still had with them. Hoover never told Americans that MacArthur refused to obey his orders. Perhaps he felt that as president, he was responsible for what had happened.

1874 Herbert Hoover is born in West Branch, Iowa, on August 10. He is the second son of Jesse and Hulda Hoover.

1880 Hoover's father dies.

1884 Hoover's mother dies. The children are separated and sent to live with relatives.

1885 After living with his Uncle Allan in West Branch, Hoover is sent to Newberg, Oregon, to live with his Uncle John Minthorn.

1888 Hoover moves with the Minthorn family to Salem, Oregon. John Minthorn opens a real estate office, and Hoover works for him.

1891 Hoover enters Stanford University, a new college in California. He begins studying to become a mining engineer.

1895 Hoover graduates from Stanford with a degree in geology.

1897 After working at several mining jobs in the West, Hoover is hired by Bewick, Moreing and Company, which sends him to Australia to oversee mining operations.

1899 Hoover marries Lou Henry, his college girlfriend. They immediately leave for Tientsin, China.

1900 Chinese rebels, known as the Boxers, revolt against their government. Their intention is to keep all things foreign out of their country. Lou and Herbert Hoover are trapped in Tientsin during the conflict, which becomes known as the Boxer Rebellion.

1901 The Hoovers move to London. Herbert Hoover is made a partner at Bewick, Moreing and Company. He and Mrs. Hoover begin traveling around the world.

1903 The Hoovers' first child, Herbert Clark Jr., is born in London.

1907 The Hoovers' second child, Allan, is born.

1908 Hoover leaves Bewick, Moreing and Company to open his own engineering firm.

1914 World War I begins. Hoover is asked to help raise money for stranded Americans who are trying to return to the United States. He also sets up food supply operations for Belgium's war victims.

1917 The United States enters World War I. President Woodrow Wilson asks Hoover to head the U.S. Food Administration.

1918 Treaties officially end World War I.

1919 Hoover leads the American Relief Administration. It continues to feed the starving people in post-war Europe. The organization feeds 350 million people in 21 countries.

1920 President Warren Harding names Hoover the secretary of commerce, a position he holds for eight years.

1927 Hoover is pictured on the first transmission of television signals.

1928 Hoover wins the presidential election, defeating New York Governor Alfred Smith.

1929 Hoover is inaugurated on March 4. He starts many building projects and adds millions of acres to the national forest and park service. President Hoover also reduces taxes for people with low incomes and creates the Federal Farm Board to help farmers. The stock market crashes on October 29. The Great Depression begins. Millions of Americans lose their jobs and homes. Many believe that President Hoover does not do enough to help.

1932 The Bonus Army marches on Washington. Hoover is severely criticized when General Douglas MacArthur breaks up the protest, although MacArthur acted without the president's orders. Franklin D. Roosevelt wins the presidential election.

1933 Herbert and Lou return to their home in Palo Alto, California.

1934 The Hoovers take an apartment in New York at the Waldorf Astoria Hotel.

1944 Lou Henry Hoover dies on January 7 in their New York apartment.

1945 President Roosevelt dies. Vice president Harry S. Truman is sworn in as president.

1946 President Harry Truman names Hoover the head of the war relief effort following the end of World War II. Hoover travels to Europe to see how he can help the citizens of war-torn nations.

1947 Hoover is appointed to head the Hoover Commission to control government spending.

1953 President Eisenhower appoints Hoover to chair the second Hoover Commission to reorganize the government.

1962 The Hoover Presidential Library and Museum opens in West Branch, Iowa, on August 10, Hoover's 88th birthday.

1964 Herbert Hoover dies on October 20 in New York.

allies (AL-lize)
Allies are nations that have agreed to help each other by fighting together against a common enemy. The U.S. Food Administration was responsible for supplying food to U.S. allies in World War I.

aviation (ay-vee-AY-shun)
Aviation is the science of flying airplanes. Aviation was a new field when Hoover was the secretary of commerce.

commerce (KOM-urss)
Commerce is the buying and selling of goods. Hoover was the secretary of commerce in the 1920s, in charge of the nation's business affairs.

conservation (kon-sur-VAY-shun)
Conservation is the act of using something carefully so that it does not run out. Hoover set up a conservation plan to make sure there would not be a shortage of food during World War I.

democracy (deh-MOK-reh-see)
A democracy is a country in which the government is run by the people who live there. The United States is a democracy.

economy (ee-KON-uh-mee)
An economy is the way money is earned and spent in a country. In the 1920s, the economy was strong, and American companies made a lot of money.

humanitarian (hyoo-man-uh-TAIR-ee-un)
A humanitarian is a person who cares for the welfare of others. Hoover was a humanitarian.

inauguration (ih-nawg-yuh-RAY-shun)
An inauguration is the ceremony that takes place when a new president begins a term. Hoover's inauguration took place on March 4, 1929.

incomes (IN-kumz)
People's incomes are the amounts of money that they earn. Hoover lowered taxes for people with low incomes.

investors (in-VES-turz)
Investors are people who use money to buy something that they hope will make a profit, such as stock. Investors in the stock market lost money during the Great Depression.

**political parties
(puh-LIT-uh-kul PAR-teez)**
Political parties are groups of people who share similar ideas about how to run a government. Hoover belonged to the Republican political party.

politics (PAWL-uh-tiks)
Politics refers to the actions and practices of the government. Politics can also be peoples' opinions about how a government should be run. Hoover said the United States should help starving people in Germany after World War I, even if their politics were different from American politics.

profit (PROF-it)
Profit is money gained from a business or an investment. People who put their money into the stock market in the 1920s hoped to make a profit.

prosperity (pros-PAIR-ih-tee)
Prosperity is success or good fortune. The 1920s were a time of prosperity because Americans earned high wages and spent a lot of money.

rebels (REB-ulz)
Rebels are people who fight against their government or other people in power. A group of Chinese rebels started the Boxer Rebellion.

stock market (STOK MAR-kit)
The stock market is where people buy and sell small pieces of ownership in different companies. These pieces are called "shares" or "stock." Companies share their profits with people who own their stock.

technology (tek-NAWL-uh-gee)
Technology is the use of scientific knowledge to create things that improve people's lives, such as telephones or computers. Aviation was a new form of technology when Hoover was the secretary of commerce.

vaccinations (vak-sih-NAY-shunz)
A vaccination is a shot or medication that protects people from disease. Hoover wanted young children to receive vaccinations.

veterans (VET-er-enz)
Veterans are people who have served in the military, especially during a war. Veterans of World War I were promised bonus money for fighting in the war.

President	Birthplace	Life Span	Presidency	Political Party	First Lady
George Washington	Virginia	1732–1799	1789–1797	None	Martha Dandridge Custis Washington
John Adams	Massachusetts	1735–1826	1797–1801	Federalist	Abigail Smith Adams
Thomas Jefferson	Virginia	1743–1826	1801–1809	Democratic-Republican	widower
James Madison	Virginia	1751–1836	1809–1817	Democratic Republican	Dolley Payne Todd Madison
James Monroe	Virginia	1758–1831	1817–1825	Democratic Republican	Elizabeth Kortright Monroe
John Quincy Adams	Massachusetts	1767–1848	1825–1829	Democratic-Republican	Louisa Johnson Adams
Andrew Jackson	South Carolina	1767–1845	1829–1837	Democrat	widower
Martin Van Buren	New York	1782–1862	1837–1841	Democrat	widower
William H. Harrison	Virginia	1773–1841	1841	Whig	Anna Symmes Harrison
John Tyler	Virginia	1790–1862	1841–1845	Whig	Letitia Christian Tyler / Julia Gardiner Tyler
James K. Polk	North Carolina	1795–1849	1845–1849	Democrat	Sarah Childress Polk

Our Presidents

President	Birthplace	Life Span	Presidency	Political Party	First Lady
Zachary Taylor	Virginia	1784–1850	1849–1850	Whig	Margaret Mackall Smith Taylor
Millard Fillmore	New York	1800–1874	1850–1853	Whig	Abigail Powers Fillmore
Franklin Pierce	New Hampshire	1804–1869	1853–1857	Democrat	Jane Means Appleton Pierce
James Buchanan	Pennsylvania	1791–1868	1857–1861	Democrat	never married
Abraham Lincoln	Kentucky	1809–1865	1861–1865	Republican	Mary Todd Lincoln
Andrew Johnson	North Carolina	1808–1875	1865–1869	Democrat	Eliza McCardle Johnson
Ulysses S. Grant	Ohio	1822–1885	1869–1877	Republican	Julia Dent Grant
Rutherford B. Hayes	Ohio	1822–1893	1877–1881	Republican	Lucy Webb Hayes
James A. Garfield	Ohio	1831–1881	1881	Republican	Lucretia Rudolph Garfield
Chester A. Arthur	Vermont	1829–1886	1881–1885	Republican	widower
Grover Cleveland	New Jersey	1837–1908	1885–1889	Democrat	Frances Folsom Cleveland

Our PRESIDENTS

President	Birthplace	Life Span	Presidency	Political Party	First Lady
Benjamin Harrison	Ohio	1833–1901	1889–1893	Republican	Caroline Scott Harrison
Grover Cleveland	New Jersey	1837–1908	1893–1897	Democrat	Frances Folsom Cleveland
William McKinley	Ohio	1843–1901	1897–1901	Republican	Ida Saxton McKinley
Theodore Roosevelt	New York	1858–1919	1901–1909	Republican	Edith Kermit Carow Roosevelt
William H. Taft	Ohio	1857–1930	1909–1913	Republican	Helen Herron Taft
Woodrow Wilson	Virginia	1856–1924	1913–1921	Democrat	Ellen L. Axson Wilson Edith Bolling Galt Wilson
Warren G. Harding	Ohio	1865–1923	1921–1923	Republican	Florence Kling De Wolfe Harding
Calvin Coolidge	Vermont	1872–1933	1923–1929	Republican	Grace Goodhue Coolidge
Herbert C. Hoover	Iowa	1874–1964	1929–1933	Republican	Lou Henry Hoover
Franklin D. Roosevelt	New York	1882–1945	1933–1945	Democrat	Anna Eleanor Roosevelt Roosevelt
Harry S. Truman	Missouri	1884–1972	1945–1953	Democrat	Elizabeth Wallace Truman

Our PRESIDENTS

President	Birthplace	Life Span	Presidency	Political Party	First Lady
Dwight D. Eisenhower	Texas	1890–1969	1953–1961	Republican	Mary "Mamie" Doud Eisenhower
John F. Kennedy	Massachusetts	1917–1963	1961–1963	Democrat	Jacqueline Bouvier Kennedy
Lyndon B. Johnson	Texas	1908–1973	1963–1969	Democrat	Claudia Alta Taylor Johnson
Richard M. Nixon	California	1913–1994	1969–1974	Republican	Thelma Catherine Ryan Nixon
Gerald Ford	Nebraska	1913–	1974–1977	Republican	Elizabeth "Betty" Bloomer Warren Ford
James Carter	Georgia	1924–	1977–1981	Democrat	Rosalynn Smith Carter
Ronald Reagan	Illinois	1911–	1981–1989	Republican	Nancy Davis Reagan
George Bush	Massachusetts	1924–	1989–1993	Republican	Barbara Pierce Bush
William Clinton	Arkansas	1946–	1993–2001	Democrat	Hillary Rodham Clinton
George W. Bush	Connecticut	1946–	2001–	Republican	Laura Welch Bush

Presidential FACTS

Qualifications

To run for president, a candidate must
- be at least 35 years old
- be a citizen who was born in the United States
- have lived in the United States for 14 years

Term of Office

A president's term of office is four years. No president can stay in office for more than two terms.

Election Date

The presidential election takes place every four years on the first Tuesday of November.

Inauguration Date

Presidents are inaugurated on January 20.

Oath of Office

I do solemnly swear I will faithfully execute the office of the President of the United States and will to the best of my ability preserve, protect, and defend the Constitution of the United States.

Write a Letter to the President

One of the best things about being a U.S. citizen is that Americans get to participate in their government. They can speak out if they feel government leaders aren't doing their jobs. They can also praise leaders who are going the extra mile. Do you have something you'd like the president to do? Should the president worry more about the environment and encourage people to recycle? Should the government spend more money on our schools? You can write a letter to the president to say how you feel!

1600 Pennsylvania Avenue
Washington, D.C. 20500

You can even send an e-mail to: president@whitehouse.gov

For Further INFORMATION

Internet Sites

Visit the Herbert Hoover Presidential Library and Museum:
http://www.hoover.nara.gov/welcome.html

Learn more about the Hoover Dam:
http://www.infoplease.com/ce5/CE024382.html

Learn more about the Great Depression:
http://www.amatecon.com/greatdepression.html

Learn more about World War I:
http://www.worldwar1.com/index.html

Learn more about all the presidents and visit the White House:
http://www.whitehouse.gov/WH/glimpse/presidents/html/presidents.html
http://www.thepresidency.org/presinfo.htm
http://www.americanpresidents.org/

Books

Clinton, Susan. *Encyclopedia of Presidents: Herbert Hoover.* Chicago: Childrens Press, 1988.

Brown, Gene. *Conflict in Europe and the Great Depression.* New York: Twenty-First Century Books, 1995.

Feinberg, Barbara Silberdick. *America's First Ladies.* New York: Franklin Watts, 1998.

Gawne, Jonathan. *Over There! The American Soldier in World War I.* Philadelphia: Chelsea House, 1999.

Meltzer, Milton. *Brother Can You Spare a Dime? The Great Depression 1929–1933.* New York: Facts on File, 1991.

Stein, R. Conrad. *The Great Depression.* Chicago: Childrens Press, 1993.

Index